Little Books of Blends & Digraphs

Exploring Letter-Sound Relationships within Meaningful Content

by
Sherrill B. Flora

illustrated by
Vanessa Countryman

Publisher
Key Education Publishing Company, LLC
Minneapolis, Minnesota

CONGRATULATIONS ON YOUR PURCHASE OF A KEY EDUCATION PRODUCT!

The editors at Key Education are former teachers who bring experience, enthusiasm, and quality to each and every product. Thousands of teachers have looked to the staff at Key Education for new and innovative resources to make their work more enjoyable and rewarding. We are committed to developing educational materials that will assist teachers in building a strong and developmentally appropriate curriculum for young children.

PLAN FOR GREAT TEACHING EXPERIENCES WHEN YOU USE EDUCATIONAL MATERIALS FROM KEY EDUCATION PUBLISHING COMPANY, LLC.

CONTENTS

How To Use This Book

Little Books of Blends and Digraphs includes thirty-one reproducible storybooks consisting of twenty beginning blends, seven final blends, and four digraphs. On the final page of each storybook is a word list, pre-reading and post-reading activities, and additional activities that reinforce each story's specific blend or digraph.

Directions: Reproduce a storybook for each child. Color, cut out along the dotted lines, and staple in numerical order.

Follow all reading suggestions and activities found on the last page of the storybook.

The children in your classroom will be thrilled when they are allowed to keep and take home the storybooks that they have learned to read at school. What an easy and inexpensive way to get reading materials into the hands of children and their families. Watch the eyes of the children light up as they get to keep each new story.

Copyright Notice

Credits

Author: Sherrill B. Flora
Inside Illustrations: Vanessa Countryman
Creative Director: Mary Claire
Cover Design: Mary Eden
Editor: George C. Flora

Key Education welcomes manuscripts and product ideas from teachers. For a copy of our submission guidelines, please send a self-addressed, stamped envelope to:
Key Education Publishing Company, LLC
Acquisitions Department
9601 Newton Avenue South
Minneapolis, Minnesota 55431

ISBN: 1-933052-09-0
Little Books of Blends and Digraphs
Copyright © 2005 Key Education Publishing Company, LLC
Minneapolis, Minnesota 55431

Blake looked at the blimp.
There was a blot on the blimp.

The blizzard could block the road.
Things looked bleak!

Consonant Blend "bl" Story

Blake,
the Weatherman

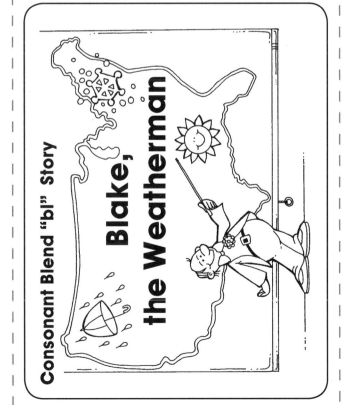

The blot meant that a blizzard
was going to blow into town.

6

Blake was blown into the blinds.

8

Notes to Teachers and Parents

DIRECTIONS TO MAKE THE BOOK: Copy the storybook for each student. Color and cut out along the dotted lines. Staple the pages together in numerical order.

BEFORE READING
1. Read the following list of "**bl**" words that appear in the story: **Blake, blimp, blot, blizzard, blow, block, bleak, blew, blast, blown, blinds, black, blue.**
2. Review any unfamiliar words in the story.

AFTER READING
1. Discuss the story. What "**bl**" words do the students remember?
2. Look through the story, then find and circle each "**bl**."

MORE "BL" ACTIVITIES
1. Blow painting: Place paper in a 13" x 9" cake pan. Drop tempera paint onto the paper. Using a straw, "blow" the paint to create an interesting design.
2. On a blackboard, or using black paper, draw a blizzard with white chalk.

5

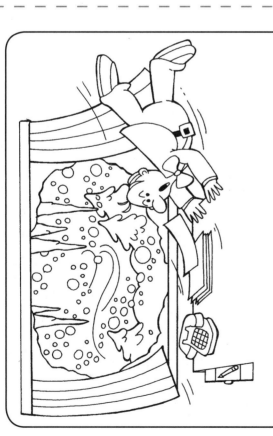

The blizzard blew in with a blast!

7

The blizzard blew away.
Blake was left black and blue.

Clyde's closet was cluttered. He had to climb over his clothes.

Clyde had to clean his closet!

Consonant Blend "cl" Story

Clyde and His Closet

Clyde could not close his closet door.

6

He gave the cloak to the clown down the street.

8

Notes to Teachers and Parents

DIRECTIONS TO MAKE THE BOOK: Copy the storybook for each student. Color and cut out along the dotted lines. Staple the pages together in numerical order.

BEFORE READING
1. Read the following list of "**cl**" words that appear in the story: **Clyde, Clyde's, closet, cluttered, clothes, climb, clean, close, clever, cloak, clown.**
2. Review any unfamiliar words in the story.

AFTER READING
1. Discuss the story. What "**cl**" words do the students remember?
2. Look through the story, then find and circle each "**cl**."

MORE "CL" ACTIVITIES
1. Make a cluttered closet. Glue one side of a piece of brown construction paper *(the closet door)* onto a white piece of paper. Fold the edge of the door so it opens. Cut out many pictures from magazines. Glue all the pictures inside the closet.
2. Draw and color a clown face.

5

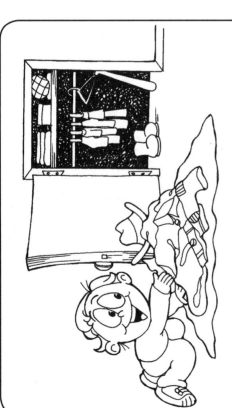

Clyde was clever.
He put his clothes in a cloak.

7

Oh no! Now the clown has a cluttered closet.

2

Flo Fly lived on top of a flagpole.

4

She flipped on her flashlight.

Consonant Blend "fl" Story

1

Flo Fly

3

One night, Flo's eyes flew open.
A big noise!

6

Flo found flea floating on a flower.

Notes to Teachers and Parents

8

DIRECTIONS TO MAKE THE BOOK: Copy the storybook for each student. Color and cut out along the dotted lines. Staple the pages together in numerical order.

BEFORE READING
1. Read the following list of "**fl**" words that appear in the story: **Flo, fly, flagpole, flipped, flashlight, flood, fled, flea, floating, flower, flew.**
2. Review any unfamiliar words in the story.

AFTER READING
1. Discuss the story. What "**fl**" words do the students remember?
2. Look through the story, then find and circle each "**fl**."

MORE "FL" ACTIVITIES
1. Floating fun: Fill a basin of water. Provide a box of objects *(bottle caps, corks, fabric, styrofoam, wood, etc...)* for the children to experiment with the concepts of "floating" and "sinking."
2. Draw a flower with Flo and flea.
3. Design a classroom or family flag.

5

Oh no! A flood!
Flo fled to find her friend flea.

7

Flo flipped flea onto her back.
They flew to safety!

Page 2

Glen was a
glimmering glowworm.

Page 4

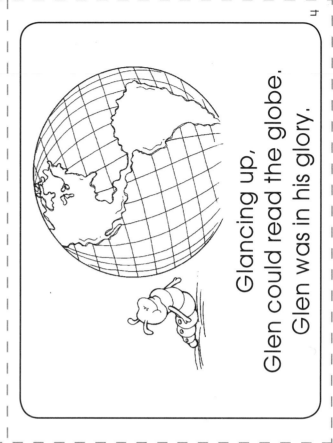

Glancing up,
Glen could read the globe.
Glen was in his glory.

Page 1

Glen Needs Glasses

Page 3

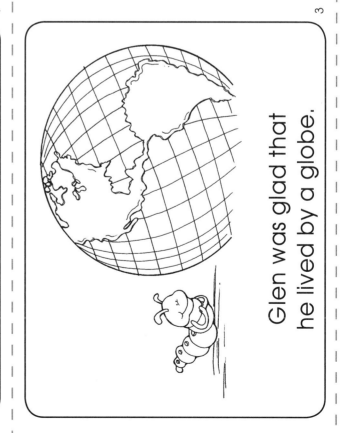

Glen was glad that
he lived by a globe.

6

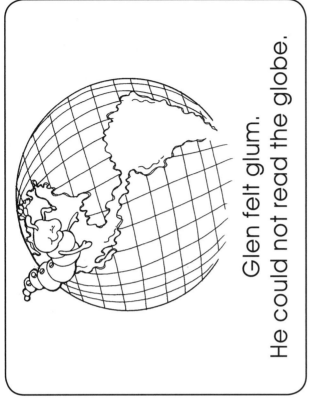

Glen felt glum.
He could not read the globe.

8

Notes to Teachers and Parents

DIRECTIONS TO MAKE THE BOOK: Copy the storybook for each student. Color and cut out along the dotted lines. Staple the pages together in numerical order.

BEFORE READING
1. Read the following list of "**gl**" words that appear in the story: **Glen, glasses, glimmering, glowworm, glad, globe, glancing, glory, glanced, glazy, glum.**
2. Review any unfamiliar words in the story.

AFTER READING
1. Discuss the story. What "**gl**" words do the students remember?
2. Look through the story, then find and circle each "**gl.**"

MORE "GL" ACTIVITIES
1. Look at a globe and find where you live.
2. Using pipecleaners, make a pair of glasses.
3. Make a list of the things that make you feel "glad."

5

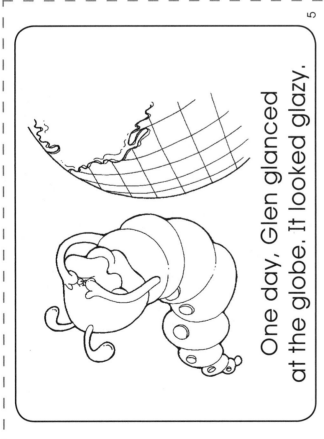

One day, Glen glanced
at the globe. It looked glazy.

7

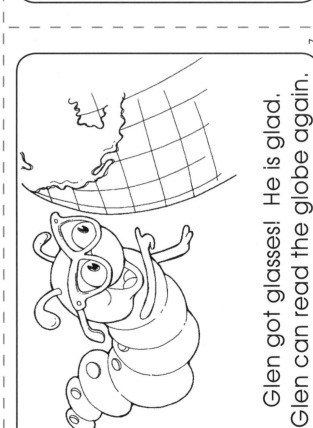

Glen got glasses! He is glad.
Glen can read the globe again.

2

Two plush toys wanted to play.

4

Then they had to plant plums.

1

Consonant Blend "pl" Story

Please! Let's Play!

3

Before they could play, they had to place the plates on the table.

KE-804009 © Key Education

11

Little Books of Blends and Digraphs

6

Oh no! The toilet was plugged.
The plunger did not work.
They had to call a plumber.

8

Notes to Teachers and Parents

DIRECTIONS TO MAKE THE BOOK: Copy the storybook for each student. Color and cut out along the dotted lines. Staple the pages together in numerical order.

BEFORE READING
1. Read the following list of "**pl**" words that appear in the story: **please, play, plush, place, plates, plant, plums, plug, plaster, plugged, plunger, plumber, playground.**
2. Review any unfamiliar words in the story.

AFTER READING
1. Discuss the story. What "**pl**" words do the students remember?
2. Look through the story, then find and circle each "**pl**."

MORE "PL" ACTIVITIES
1. Using playdough, mold a plush animal.
2. Plant some seeds in a styrofoam cup filled with dirt.
3. Learn how to fold and fly a paper plane.

5

Then the plush toys had
to plug a hole with plaster.

7

Finally, the plush toys
went to the playground.

2

Meet slug. Slug is a slippery bug.

4

Slug slid on slick sleet.

Consonant Blend "sl" Story

What a Slippery Day!

1

3

Slug loves to slip and slide.

6

Slug sleds down the slopes.

8

Notes to Teachers and Parents

DIRECTIONS TO MAKE THE BOOK: Copy the storybook for each student. Color and cut out along the dotted lines. Staple the pages together in numerical order.

BEFORE READING

1. Read the following list of "**sl**" words that appear in the story: **slippery, slug, slip, slips, slide, slides, slid, slick, sleet, slush, sleds, slopes, sleep.**

2. Review any unfamiliar words in the story.

AFTER READING

1. Discuss the story. What "**sl**" words do the students remember?

2. Look through the story, then find and circle each "**sl**."

MORE "SL" ACTIVITIES

1. Make "slime." Take 2 parts white glue and mix with 1 part liquid starch. If too thick add more starch. This is really fun to play with.

2. Make a sled using craft sticks.

3. Discover what a real "slug" looks like.

5

Slug slides in the slush.

7

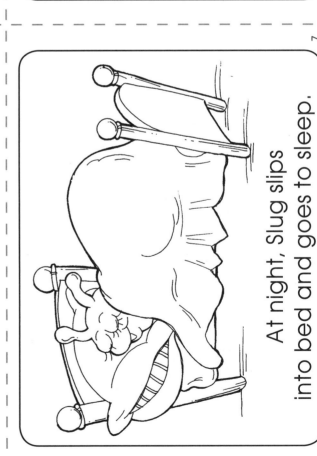

At night, Slug slips into bed and goes to sleep.

Brad and Brent were brothers.

Brave Brad would brag
that he could ride a bronco.

Consonant Blend "br" Story

Brad and Brent

Brad was brave. Brent had brains.

6

The bronco bucked Brad off.
A breeze broke Brent's bridge.

8

Notes to Teachers and Parents

DIRECTIONS TO MAKE THE BOOK: Copy the storybook for each student. Color and cut out along the dotted lines. Staple the pages together in numerical order.

BEFORE READING

1. Read the following list of "**br**" words that appear in the story:
   Brad, Brent, brothers, brave, brains, brag, bronco, brainy, bridge, breeze, broke, Brent's, bragging.
2. Review any unfamiliar words in the story.

AFTER READING

1. Discuss the story. What "**br**" words do the students remember?
2. Look through the story, then find and circle each "**br**."

MORE "BR" ACTIVITIES

1. Use a 1" x 7" piece of white construction paper to design a bracelet. Tape the ends together to fit.
2. Build a bridge using blocks, craft sticks, or Lego's™.

5

Brainy Brent would brag
that he could build a bridge.

7

The brothers are done bragging.

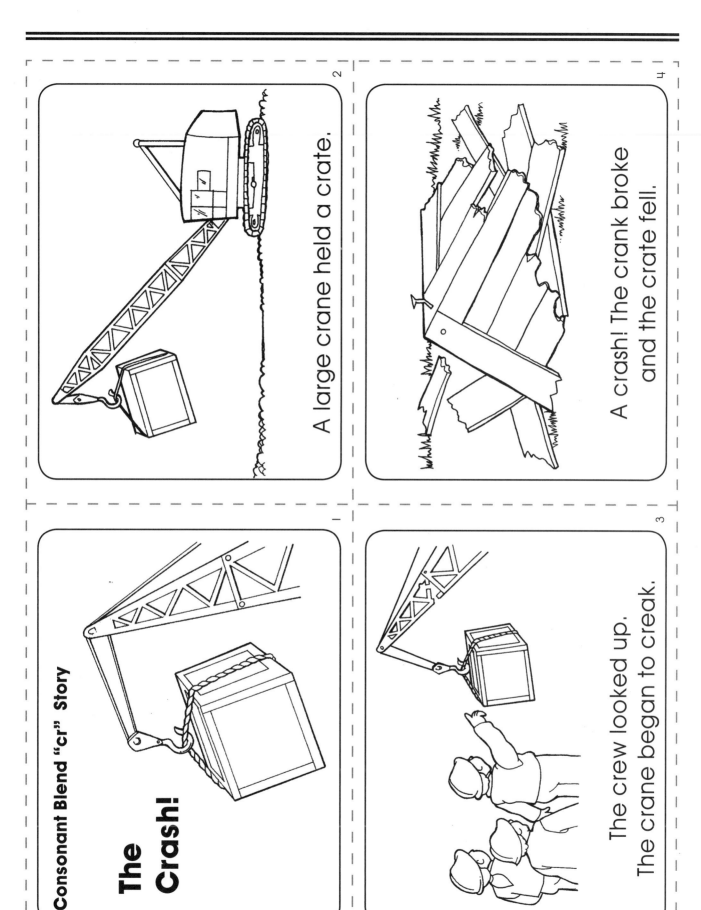

Consonant Blend "cr" Story

The Crash!

A large crane held a crate.

The crew looked up.
The crane began to creak.

A crash! The crank broke
and the crate fell.

2

4

1

3

6

The crew said, "That critter was lucky not to be crushed!"

8

Notes to Teachers and Parents

DIRECTIONS TO MAKE THE BOOK: Copy the storybook for each student. Color and cut out along the dotted lines. Staple the pages together in numerical order.

BEFORE READING

1. Read the following list of "**cr**" words that appear in the story: **crash, crane, crate, crew, creak, crank, cry, crawled, cricket, critter, crushed, crutches.**

2. Review any unfamiliar words in the story.

AFTER READING

1. Discuss the story. What "**cr**" words do the students remember?

2. Look through the story, then find and circle each "**cr**."

MORE "CR" ACTIVITIES

1. Use color crayons to draw a picture of the cricket.

2. Design a crown. Use sequins, buttons, foil, and glitter.

5

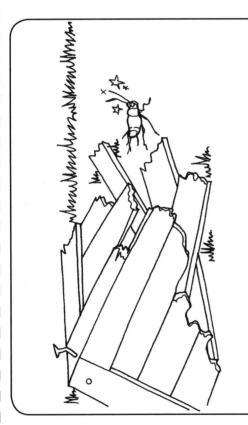

Under the crate came a cry.
Out crawled a cricket.

7

The crew made crutches
for the cricket.

Once there was a dragon.
He dreamed of drifting on water.

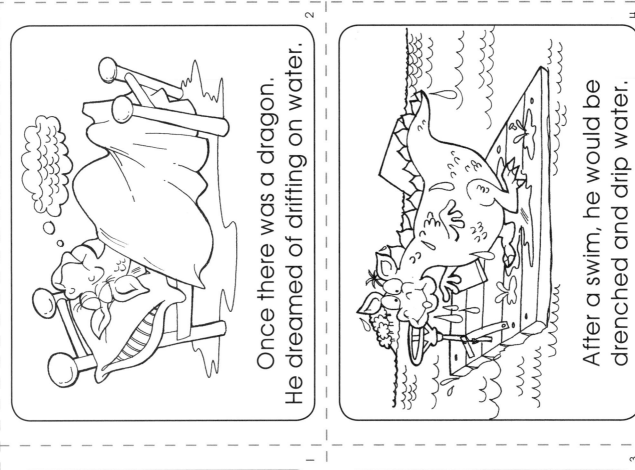

After a swim, he would be
drenched and drip water.

Consonant Blend "dr" Story

**The
Dragon's
Dream**

In his dream, he would drift
on a raft and drink lemonade.

Little Books of Blends and Digraphs

6

Finally, the dragon would drive his raft home.

8

Notes to Teachers and Parents

DIRECTIONS TO MAKE THE BOOK: Copy the storybook for each student. Color and cut out along the dotted lines. Staple the pages together in numerical order.

BEFORE READING
1. Read the following list of "**dr**" words that appear in the story: **dragon, dragon's, dream, dreamed, drift, drifting, drink, drenched, drip, dry, dress, drive, drown.**
2. Review any unfamiliar words in the story.

AFTER READING
1. Discuss the story. What "**dr**" words do the students remember?
2. Look through the story, then find and circle each "**dr**."

MORE "DR" ACTIVITIES
1. Draw a picture of what you think a dragon should look like.
2. Can you remember one of your dreams? Share a dream.
3. Sample some dried fruit: raisins, cranberries, bananas, or apples.

5

He would dry off and dress in a robe.

7

The dragon woke up and cried, "I would drown! I don't know how to swim!"

Fred Frog had a terrible fright!

With a frown, Fran said,
"Do not fret."

Consonant Blend "fr" Story

Fred Frog's Fright!

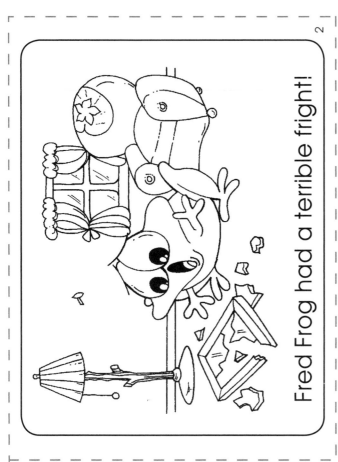

He ran to his friend's house.
Her name is Fran.
Fred stood frozen in fear!

 Little Books of Blends and Digraphs

6

What made the frame fall?
They went back to Fred's house.

8

Notes to Teachers and Parents

DIRECTIONS TO MAKE THE BOOK: Copy the storybook for each student. Color and cut out along the dotted lines. Staple the pages together in numerical order.

BEFORE READING
1. Read the following list of "**fr**" words that appear in the story:
Fred, Fred's, frog's, frog, fright, Fran, friend's, frozen, frown, fret, frigid, frame, frisbee, fright.
2. Review any unfamiliar words in the story.

AFTER READING
1. Discuss the story. What "**fr**" words do the students remember?
2. Look through the story, then find and circle each "**fr**."

MORE "FR" ACTIVITIES
1. Draw a picture of Fred and Fran. Bend the corners of the picture to create a frame.
2. Sample some fresh fruit.
3. Go outside and play with a frisbee.

5

Fred was frigid.
He told Fran a frame had fallen.

7

"Oh look," said Fran,
"A frisbee hit the frame. There is no reason to be frozen in fright!"

2

Grumpy grandfather grasshopper was growling. He was so hungry.

4

The grasshoppers went to the grocery store.

The Grasshoppers

1

3

Grandmother grasshopper groaned, "Don't be a grouch!"

6

Grandmother had grapes.

8

Notes to Teachers and Parents

DIRECTIONS TO MAKE THE BOOK: Copy the storybook for each student. Color and cut out along the dotted lines. Staple the pages together in numerical order.

BEFORE READING
1. Read the following list of "**gr**" words that appear in the story: **grasshoppers, grasshopper, grumpy, grandfather, grandmother, growling, groaned, grouch, grocery, grass, grapes, grill, great, grin.**
2. Review any unfamiliar words in the story.

AFTER READING
1. Discuss the story. What "**gr**" words do the students remember?
2. Look through the story, then find and circle each "**gr.**"

MORE "GR" ACTIVITIES
1. Draw a picture of your grandparents and send it to them.
2. Draw two faces. Make one face with a grin and the other face looking grumpy.
3. Write a grocery list. What things would you like to buy at the grocery store.

5

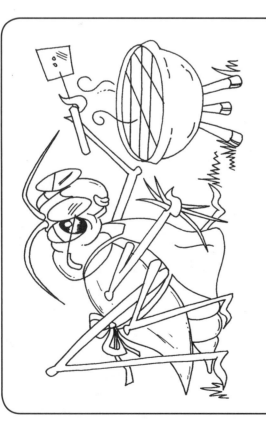

Grandfather got grass to grill.

7

There was no more growling.
Grandfather had a great big grin.

2

Princess Priscilla wanted to marry a prince.

4

The problem was the winner had to prove he was a prince.

1

Consonant Blend "pr" Story

Princess Priscilla

3

CONTEST TO MARRY PRINCESS

There would be a contest. The prize would be Princess Priscilla.

6

One gave her praise.
One gave her a pretzel.

8

Notes to Teachers and Parents

DIRECTIONS TO MAKE THE BOOK: Copy the storybook for each student. Color and cut out along the dotted lines. Staple the pages together in numerical order.

BEFORE READING
1. Read the following list of "**pr**" words that appear in the story: **Princess, Priscilla, prince, problem, prove, prize, present, praise, pretzel, proved, precious.**
2. Review any unfamiliar words in the story.

AFTER READING
1. Discuss the story. What "**pr**" words do the students remember?
2. Look through the story, then find and circle each "**pr**."

MORE "PR" ACTIVITIES
1. If you could win a contest, what would you like your prize to be?
2. Make prints. Cut sponges into various shapes. Dip the sponges into tempera paint and press them onto paper.
3. Make a pretzel log cabin. Glue stick pretzels on paper to create the shape of a cabin. Glue smaller pretzels inside the shape to finish the inside of the cabin.

5

Each prince brought
Princess Priscilla a present.

7

One proved he was a prince.
He said, "Princess Priscilla
you are precious."

The triplets wanted to travel by train.

The train came down the tracks. It stopped under the tree.

Consonant Blend "tr" Story

Traveling by Train

They packed their trunks. Then they trotted off to the train.

6

They ate treats on the train.

8

Notes to Teachers and Parents

DIRECTIONS TO MAKE THE BOOK: Copy the storybook for each student. Color and cut out along the dotted lines. Staple the pages together in numerical order.

BEFORE READING
1. Read the following list of **"tr"** words that appear in the story: **traveling, train, triplets, travel, trunks, trotted, tracks, tree, trio, trip, treats, tremendous, truly.**
2. Review any unfamiliar words in the story.

AFTER READING
1. Discuss the story. What **"tr"** words do the students remember?
2. Look through the story, then find and circle each **"tr."**

MORE "TR" ACTIVITIES
1. Make a travel poster advertising a place that you would like to travel to.
2. Pretend that you found an old trunk in the attic. What do you think is in the trunk?
3. Read the story of *The Three Billy Goats Gruff.* Draw a picture of the troll.

5

The trio sat down and got ready for their trip.

7

The trip was tremendous! They had a truly great time.

Stella went to the store.
She wanted to cook stew

Stella stirred the stew.
The stew started to steam.

Consonant Blend "st" Story

Stella's Stew

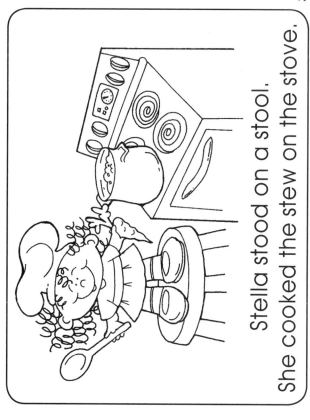

Stella stood on a stool.
She cooked the stew on the stove.

6

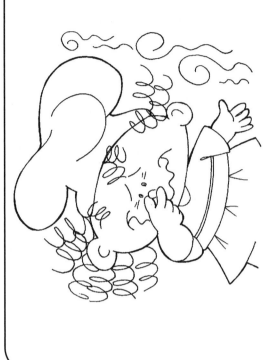

Stop cooking! Something stinks!

Notes to Teachers and Parents

DIRECTIONS TO MAKE THE BOOK: Copy the storybook for each student. Color and cut out along the dotted lines. Staple the pages together in numerical order.

BEFORE READING
1. Read the following list of "**st**" words that appear in the story: **Stella, Stella's, stew, store, stove, stood, stool, stirred, started, steam, stared, stinks, stop, stunk, stale.**
2. Review any unfamiliar words in the story.

AFTER READING
1. Discuss the story. What "**st**" words do the students remember?
2. Look through the story, then find and circle each "**st**."

MORE "ST" ACTIVITIES
1. Make your own stamps. Cut self-stick foam into shapes. Peel off the backing and stick to a wood block. Dip into paint or on an ink pad and stamp a design on paper.
2. Read *Stone Soup* and then create your own stew.

8

5

Something is wrong. Stella stared at the stew.

The stew stunk! It was stale!

7

Snib Snail had a bad cold.
He sneezed and sneezed.

During the day,
Snib would sniff and sniff.

Consonant Blend "sn" Story

Snib Snail

At night, Snib snored and snored.

6

The cold and snow gave
Snib Snail his cold.

8

Notes to Teachers and Parents

DIRECTIONS TO MAKE THE BOOK: Copy the storybook for each student. Color and cut out along the dotted lines. Staple the pages together in numerical order.

BEFORE READING
1. Read the following list of "**sn**" words that appear in the story: **Snib, Snail, sneeze, sneezed, snore, snored, sniff, snout, snow, snaps, snowshoe.**
2. Review any unfamiliar words in the story.

AFTER READING
1. Discuss the story. What "**sn**" words do the students remember?
2. Look through the story, then find and circle each "**sn**."

MORE "SN" ACTIVITIES
1. Make a snow picture. Using white paint on blue paper, create a snow scene. When the white paint is still wet, sprinkle sugar on the paint. The paint will sparkle when it dries.
2. Use white playdough and mold a snowman. Use scrap fabric to make a scarf.

5

Sneeze, snore, and sniff.
Sneeze, snore, and sniff.
His poor snout was sore.

7

Next time, Snib Snail will
snap on a snowshoe.

2

Scott the scarecrow
scanned the corn field.

4

Scott waved
a scarlet scarf at the crows.

1

Scott the Scarecrow

3

The job of a scarecrow is
to scare away the crows.

6

Scott yelled, "Crows, don't scoop up the corn!"

8

Notes to Teachers and Parents

DIRECTIONS TO MAKE THE BOOK: Copy the storybook for each student. Color and cut out along the dotted lines. Staple the pages together in numerical order.

BEFORE READING
1. Read the following list of "**sc**" words that appear in the story: **Scott, scarecrow, scare, scanned, scarlet, scarf, scat, scoop, scolded.**
2. Review any unfamiliar words in the story.

AFTER READING
1. Discuss the story. What "**sc**" words do the students remember?
2. Look through the story, then find and circle each "**sc**."

MORE "SC" ACTIVITIES
1. Draw the outline of a fish. Dip your finger in paint and press to create scales on the fish. Use a variety of colors.
2. Design your own scarecrow.

5

Scat crows!

7

Scott the scarecrow scolded the crows. They felt sorry.

Spencer's mom said,
"Come eat a special dinner."

Nothing can spoil this dinner!
I have spent hours cooking it.

Consonant Blend "sp" Story

The Special Dinner

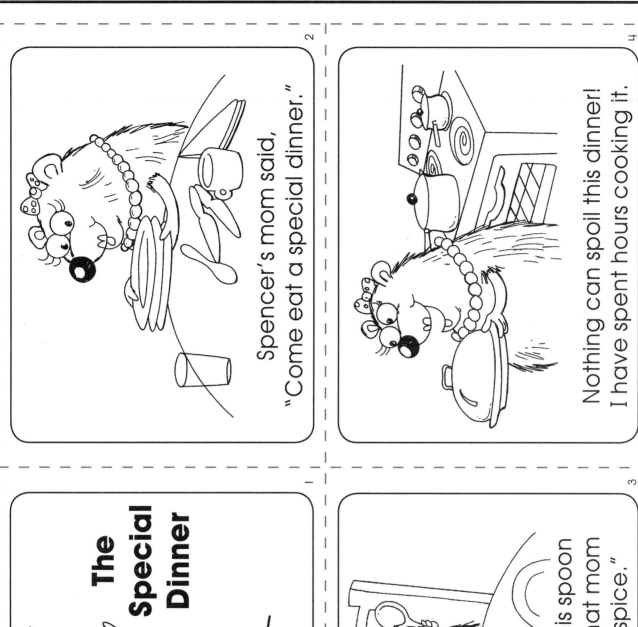

Spencer grabbed his spoon
and said, "I hope that mom
did not spare the spice."

6

With great speed, Spencer
cleaned the spot with a sponge.

8

Notes to Teachers and Parents

DIRECTIONS TO MAKE THE BOOK: Copy the storybook for each student. Color and cut out along the dotted lines. Staple the pages together in numerical order.

BEFORE READING
1. Read the following list of "**sp**" words that appear in the story: **special, Spencer, Spencer's, spoon, speed, spare, spice, spent, spoil, spilled, spot, spoiled, sponge, spinach.**
2. Review any unfamiliar words in the story.

AFTER READING
1. Discuss the story. What "**sp**" words do the students remember?
2. Look through the story, then find and circle each "**sp**."

MORE "SP" ACTIVITIES
1. Draw a picture of what you think you might see when you look out the window of a spaceship.
2. Make a wooden spoon puppet.

5

Spencer spilled! It left a spot!

7

Spencer's mom said, "Don't worry.
The spinach is not spoiled."

2

The sweet swan looked so sad.

4

Swarms of flies live in the swamp.
The swan swats the flies.

Consonant Blend "sw" Story

The Swan

1

3

The swan is sad
because she lives in a swamp!

6

The swan swam
through the swamp.
She began to sway and swirl.

8

Notes to Teachers and Parents

DIRECTIONS TO MAKE THE BOOK: Copy the storybook for each student. Color and cut out along the dotted lines. Staple the pages together in numerical order.

BEFORE READING
1. Read the following list of "**sw**" words that appear in the story: **swan, sweet, swamp, swarms, swats, swims, swam, switch, sway, swirl, swept, swell.**
2. Review any unfamiliar words in the story.

AFTER READING
1. Discuss the story. What "**sw**" words do the students remember?
2. Look through the story, then find and circle each "**sw**."

MORE "SW" ACTIVITIES
1. Make a list of all the words you can think of that begin with "**sw**."
2. Read the story of *The Ugly Duckling*.

5

The sweet swan swims away.
She must switch homes.

7

The Swan was
swept to her new home.
What a swell place!

Small Smith is a pig
and a great painter.

Small Smith would smash
paint on the paper.

Consonant Blend "sm" Story

Small
Smith

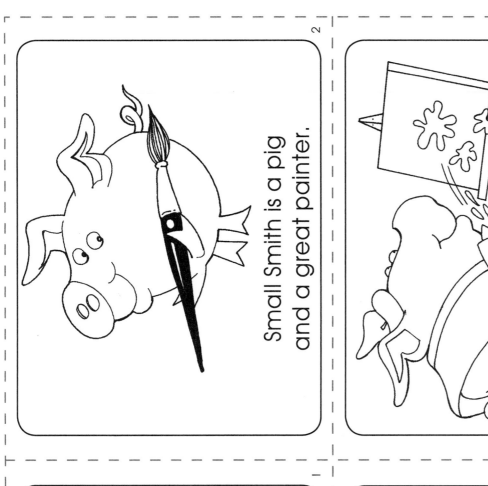

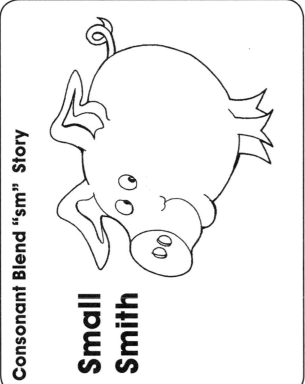

Small Smith wore a smock
and a smile when he painted.

6

Smith thought he smelled smoke.
He was smart and ran outside.

8

Notes to Teachers and Parents

DIRECTIONS TO MAKE THE BOOK: Copy the storybook for each student. Color and cut out along the dotted lines. Staple the pages together in numerical order.

BEFORE READING ----------------------------------
1. Read the following list of "**sm**" words that appear in the story: **small, Smith, smock, smile, smash, smear, smudge, smooth, smelled, smoke, smart, smiled, smog.**
2. Review any unfamiliar words in the story.

AFTER READING ----------------------------------
1. Discuss the story. What "**sm**" words do the students remember?
2. Look through the story, then find and circle each "**sm**."

MORE "SM" ACTIVITIES ----------------------------
1. Using finger paint, smear paint just like Small Smith did in the story.
2. Make a list of all the things you know that make you smart.
3. Play a "smelling" game. Blindfold and guess various smells: lemon, cinnamon, vanilla, chocolate, playdough, vinegar, etc.

5

Then he would smear and smudge the paint until it was smooth.

7

It was not smoke.
It was smog. Smith smiled.

Consonant Blend "sk" Story

The Skills
of
Skipper

Skipper was a skinny cat.
She had many skills.

Skipper could sketch
pictures of the sky.

Skipper could skip
when she roller skated.

6

Acting is a skill.
Skipper wore a skirt in a skit.

8

Notes to Teachers and Parents

DIRECTIONS TO MAKE THE BOOK: Copy the storybook for each student. Color and cut out along the dotted lines. Staple the pages together in numerical order.

BEFORE READING
1. Read the following list of "**sk**" words that appear in the story:
   Skipper, skills, skill, skinny, skip, skated, ski, skids, sky, sketch, skirt, skit, skilled, skydiving.
2. Review any unfamiliar words in the story.

AFTER READING
1. Discuss the story. What "**sk**" words do the students remember?
2. Look through the story, then find and circle each "**sk**."

MORE "SK" ACTIVITIES
1. Design your own skyscraper.
2. How many words can you spell that begin with "sk?"
3. Sketch a picture of a skateboard.

5

Skipper could ski.
She skids to a stop.

7

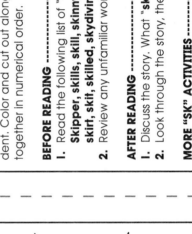

Her favorite skill is skydiving!
What a skilled skinny cat.

42

2

Bang the gong!
Here comes the young king!

4

Ring the bells!
Here comes the young king!

The Young King

1

3

Sing the song!
Here comes the young king!

6

The bong was gonged.
The song was sung.
The bells were rung.

8

Notes to Teachers and Parents

DIRECTIONS TO MAKE THE BOOK: Copy the storybook for each student. Color and cut out along the dotted lines. Staple the pages together in numerical order.

BEFORE READING
1. Read the following list of "**–ng**" words that appear in the story: **young, king, bang, gong, sing, song, ring, wrong, bong, sung, rung, swing, swung.**
2. Review any unfamiliar words in the story.

AFTER READING
1. Discuss the story. What "**–ng**" words do the students remember?
2. Look through the story, then find and circle each "**–ng**."

MORE "–NG" ACTIVITIES
1. Make a list of your favorite songs.
2. The king came in on a swing. Design and draw the perfect swingset.

5

What is wrong?

7

The young king
swung in on a swing.
The crowd was stunned!

2

Frank wanted to play
a prank on Hank.

4

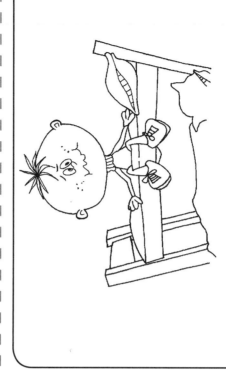

Frank was blank!
He could not think of a prank.
Then he got an idea!

1

Frank and Hank

3

Frank sank into his bunk
and began to think.

6

Hank came in to have a drink.
"Don't drink!" yelled Frank.
"I shrunk and fell in your drink."

8

Notes to Teachers and Parents

DIRECTIONS TO MAKE THE BOOK: Copy the storybook for each student. Color and cut out along the dotted lines. Staple the pages together in numerical order.

BEFORE READING
1. Read the following list of "**–nk**" words that appear in the story: **Frank, Hank, prank, sank, bunk, think, blank, junk, trunk, drink, shrunk, shrink.**
2. Review any unfamiliar words in the story.

AFTER READING
1. Discuss the story. What "**–nk**" words do the students remember?
2. Look through the story, then find and circle each "**–nk**."

MORE "–nk" ACTIVITIES
1. How many words can you rhyme with ink?
2. Have you ever played a prank on someone? Has anyone ever played a prank on you?
3. Draw a picture of a pink piggy bank.

5

Frank took the junk
out of the trunk and hid.

7

Hank said, "How did you shrink?
I don't think you shrunk!
I think it is a prank."

Hound dog is the
leader of the band.

Listen to the sound. He waves
the wand 'round and 'round.

Ending Consonant Blend "–nd" Story

Hound
Dog
and
the
Band

Hound dog holds
the wand in his hand.

6

Bug said, "Lend me your wand.
Let me lead the band!"

8

Notes to Teachers and Parents

DIRECTIONS TO MAKE THE BOOK: Copy the storybook for each student. Color and cut out along the dotted lines. Staple the pages together in numerical order.

BEFORE READING
1. Read the following list of "–nd" words that appear in the story: **Hound, band, hand, wand, sound, 'round, and, kind, fond, lend, found, stand.**
2. Review any unfamiliar words in the story.

AFTER READING
1. Discuss the story. What "–nd" words do the students remember?
2. Look through the story, then find and circle each "–nd."

MORE "–ND" ACTIVITIES
1. Make sand jars. Pour colored sand *(available at most craft stores)* into small jars. Layer the colors by alternating various colors of sand.
2. Make a wind sock by coloring a design on a 12" x 18" piece of paper and then roll it into a tube. Tape streamers to the bottom. Attach string to the top so it can hang.

5

A kind little bug
was fond of the band.

7

Hound found a way to help bug.
He said, "Stand on my head!"

2

The ant bent down.
He picked up a cent.

4

How should the cent be spent?
You could rent a tent.

Ant and the Cent

1

3

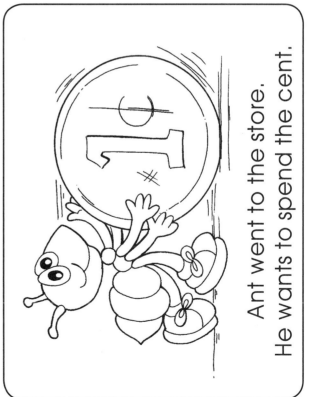

Ant went to the store.
He wants to spend the cent.

6

How about a bunt cake?
I grant you will love it.

Notes to Teachers and Parents

DIRECTIONS TO MAKE THE BOOK: Copy the storybook for each student. Color and cut out along the dotted lines. Staple the pages together in numerical order.

BEFORE READING
1. Read the following list of "**–nt**" words that appear in the story:
   ant, bent, cent, want, went, spent, rent, tent, mint, plant, scent, bunt, grant.
2. Review any unfamiliar words in the story.

AFTER READING
1. Discuss the story. What "**–nt**" words do the students remember?
2. Look through the story, then find and circle each "**–nt**."

MORE "–NT" ACTIVITIES
1. Pudding Finger Paint. Mix the pudding according to the directions on the package. Use on finger paint paper.
2. Cent Rubbings. Lay a coin under a thin sheet of paper. Hold the crayon on its side and rub it back and forth until you see the details of the coin appear on the paper.

8

5

How about a mint plant?
You will love the scent.

7

Ant went home.
Ant saved the cent.

2

Wisp was a little wasp
who could not fly.

4

"Gasp!" Wisp yelled,
"I must clasp onto my house."

Ending Consonant Blend "–sp" Story

Wisp the Wasp

3

One crisp morning, Wisp tried to fly.

6

Wisp's friend handed
him a string to grasp.

8

Notes to Teachers and Parents

DIRECTIONS TO MAKE THE BOOK: Copy the storybook for each student. Color and cut out along the dotted lines. Staple the pages together in numerical order.

BEFORE READING
1. Read the following list of "**–sp**" words that appear in the story:
   Wisp, wasp, gasp, clasp, crisp, grasp.
2. Review any unfamiliar words in the story.

AFTER READING
1. Discuss the story. What "**–sp**" words do the students remember?
2. Look through the story, then find and circle each "**–sp**."

MORE "–SP" ACTIVITIES
1. Make apple crisp.
2. Wasps and bees make honey. Let the children sample honey on bread, corn muffins, or crackers.

5

I cannot lose my grasp!

7

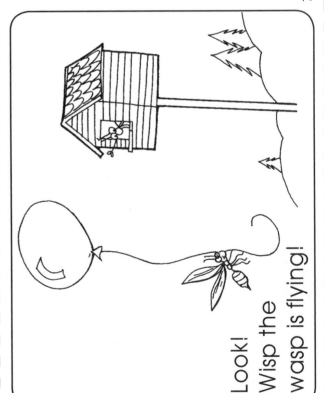

Look!
Wisp the
wasp is flying!

Ending Consonant Blend "-sk" Story

Ellie's
Big
Task

1

Ellie sat at her desk.
She had a big task to do.

2

She worked from dawn to dusk.

3

Ellie's friends said, "Take a risk!
Ask Ellie what she is doing."

4

Little Books of Blends and Digraphs

6

My task is to make each of you a mask.

8

Notes to Teachers and Parents

DIRECTIONS TO MAKE THE BOOK: Copy the storybook for each student. Color and cut out along the dotted lines. Staple the pages together in numerical order.

BEFORE READING
1. Read the following list of "**–sk**" words that appear in the story:
   desk, task, dusk, ask, risk, tisk, mask, tusks.
2. Review any unfamiliar words in the story.

AFTER READING
1. Discuss the story. What "**–sk**" words do the students remember?
2. Look through the story, then find and circle each "**–sk**."

MORE "–SK" ACTIVITIES
1. Use a paper plate and create your own mask. Tape a paint stir stick or a craft stick to the bottom of the plate so it can be held in front of the face.
2. Make a list of all the things that you could find in a desk.
3. Draw a picture of your backyard at dusk.

5

"Tisk, tisk, tisk," said Ellie. "Don't spy, just ask me."

7

Now each of you have elephant tusks.

Hello. Please be my guest at the best hotel.

There is no dust and each meal is a feast.

Ending Consonant Blend "–st" Story

Be My Guest

Trust me! I am honest. This hotel is first rate.

6

No jest!
You are my host. I am the guest!

8

Notes to Teachers and Parents

DIRECTIONS TO MAKE THE BOOK: Copy the storybook for each student. Color and cut out along the dotted lines. Staple the pages together in numerical order.

BEFORE READING
1. Read the following list of "**–st**" words that appear in the story: **guest, best, trust, honest, first, dust, feast, fast, list, jest, host, cost, contest, blast.**
2. Review any unfamiliar words in the story.

AFTER READING
1. Discuss the story. What "**–st**" words do the students remember?
2. Look through the story, then find and circle each "**–st**."

MORE "–ST" ACTIVITIES
1. Use a stop watch and time how "fast" you can run.
2. If you could design a contest, what would the prize be?
3. If you won a contest, who would you invite to be your guests?

5

Please, get here fast.
Our names are on the list.

7

There is no cost.
I won a contest. What a blast!

2

Chad was a chipmunk.
He wanted to be a champ.

4

Chimp said, "Chew on cheese and cherries and you could become a champ."

Consonant Digraph "ch" Story

Can Chad Be A Champ?

1

3

Chad went to see Chimp the Chef. Chad asked Chimp to help him change his diet.

6

The crowd cheered as the animals charged ahead. Who will be the champ?

8

Notes to Teachers and Parents

DIRECTIONS TO MAKE THE BOOK: Copy the storybook for each student. Color and cut out along the dotted lines. Staple the pages together in numerical order.

BEFORE READING
1. Read the following list of "**ch**" words that appear in the story: **Chad, chipmunk, champ, chef, chimp, change, chew, cheese, cherries, cheetah, chasing, cheered, charged, chuckled, chance.**
2. Review any unfamiliar words in the story.

AFTER READING
1. Discuss the story. What "**ch**" words do the students remember?
2. Look through the story, then find and circle each "**ch**."

MORE "CH" ACTIVITIES
1. Learn how to play checkers.
2. Have a cheese sampling party.
3. Write a poem about baby chicks. Include the word "cheep."

5

Chad then went to see Cheetah. Cheetah trained Chad to run fast by chasing him.

7

Chad chuckled! He took a chance. Now he was the champ!

2

The boy on the ship shouted, "I see a shape in the water!"

4

"Shape, show yourself! Share who you are!" shouted the boy.

Consonant Digraph "sh" Story

1

The Shy Shark

3

The boy shook and shivered. He was in shock.

6

She is a shark! The shark shook and said, "Shame on you for making me shiver."

Notes to Teachers and Parents

DIRECTIONS TO MAKE THE BOOK: Copy the storybook for each student. Color and cut out along the dotted lines. Staple the pages together in numerical order.

BEFORE READING
1. Read the following list of "**sh**" words that appear in the story: **shy, shark, ship, shouted, shape, shook, shivered, shock, show, share, shot, she, shred, shame, shiver.**
2. Review any unfamiliar words in the story.

AFTER READING
1. Discuss the story. What "**sh**" words do the students remember?
2. Look through the story, then find and circle each "**sh**."

MORE "SH" ACTIVITIES
1. Draw an outline of a sheep. Brush white glue inside the sheep outline. Press cotton to create a soft, woolly sheep.
2. Draw a picture of the shy shark.
3. What is something that would make you shiver and shake?

8

5

A head shot out of the water. The shape did not have a shred of courage.

The boy said, "I am in shock! A shy shark."

7

2

There you are.
I thought you had left.

4

Your throat looks thick.
Is it throbbing?

Consonant Digraph "th" Story

I Think I Am Sick

1

3

I did not go. I think I am sick.
Look at my throat.

6

I will get you through this.
Drink this!

8

Notes to Teachers and Parents

DIRECTIONS TO MAKE THE BOOK: Copy the storybook for each student. Color and cut out along the dotted lines. Staple the pages together in numerical order.

BEFORE READING
1. Read the following list of "**th**" words that appear in the story: **there, thought, think, throat, thick, throbbing, throbs, thirsty, through, this, thrill, thank.**
2. Review any unfamiliar words in the story.

AFTER READING
1. Discuss the story. What "**th**" words do the students remember?
2. Look through the story, then find and circle each "**th**."

MORE "TH" ACTIVITIES
1. Draw a picture of the Three Pigs and the Three Bears.
2. Make a list of all the words you know that begin with "**th**."
3. Go outside and practice throwing a ball.

5

Oh yes, it throbs. I am so thirsty.

7

What a thrill! I feel better.
Thank you!

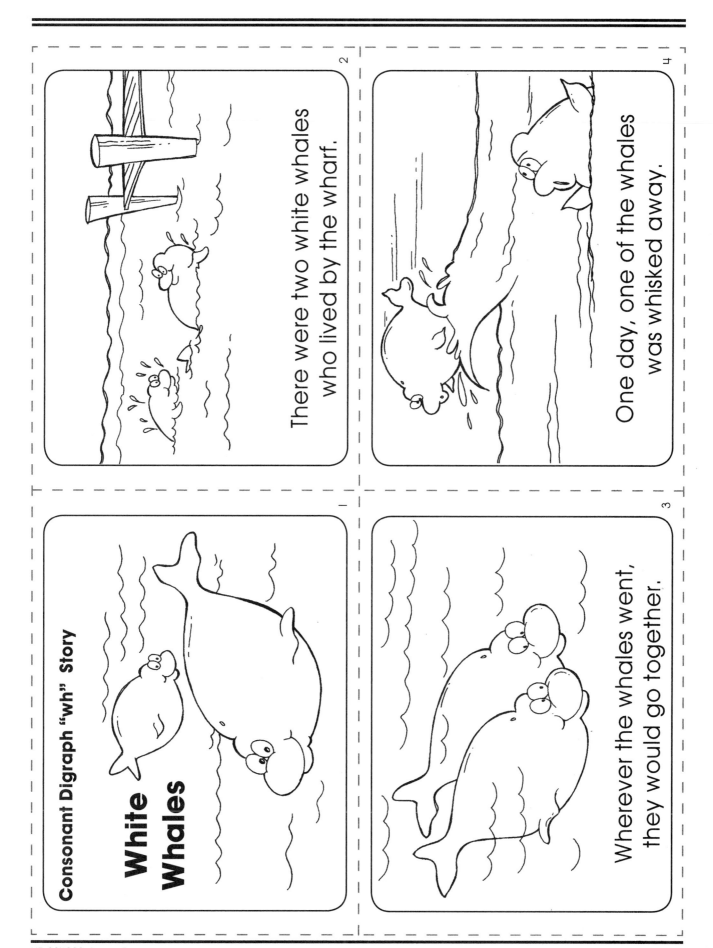

Consonant Digraph "wh" Story

White Whales

There were two white whales who lived by the wharf.

2

Wherever the whales went, they would go together.

3

One day, one of the whales was whisked away.

4

1

63

6

The whale whined
and whimpered.
Which way should I go?

8

Notes to Teachers and Parents

DIRECTIONS TO MAKE THE BOOK: Copy the storybook for each student. Color and cut out along the dotted lines. Staple the pages together in numerical order.

BEFORE READING
1. Read the following list of "**wh**" words that appear in the story: **whale, whales, wharf, white, who, where, what, why, whined, which, whimpered, wherever, whisked, whoa, whistle.**
2. Review any unfamiliar words in the story.

AFTER READING
1. Discuss the story. What "**wh**" words do the students remember?
2. Look through the story, then find and circle each "**wh**."

MORE "WH" ACTIVITIES
1. Play telephone by whispering a sentence into the ear of the person sitting next to you and have them pass it on.
2. Make a list of the things that you could put in a wheelbarrow.
3. Pretend you are a reporter. Interview a friend and remember to ask, "who, what, when, where, and why."

5

What happened?
Where am I?
Why am I lost?

7

Whoa! A whistle!
The whale has found her friend.